THE
INSTRUCTION OF
PTAH-HOTEP AND THE
INSTRUCTION OF KE'GEMNI

THE OLDEST BOOKS IN THE WORLD
(1908)

Translated by:
Battiscombe G. Gunn

ISBN 0-7661-0131-2

The Wisdom of the East Series

EDITED BY

L. CRANMER-BYNG

Dr. S. A. KAPADIA

THE INSTRUCTION OF PTAH-HOTEP

WISDOM OF THE EAST

THE INSTRUCTION OF PTAH-HOTEP AND THE INSTRUCTION OF KE'GEMNI: THE OLDEST BOOKS IN THE WORLD

TRANSLATED FROM THE EGYPTIAN
WITH AN INTRODUCTION AND APPENDIX
BY BATTISCOMBE G. GUNN

NEW YORK
E. P. DUTTON AND COMPANY
1908

TO

MY MOTHER

VII. NOV. MCMIV

CONTENTS

EDITORIAL NOTE

THE object of the editors of this series is a very definite one. They desire above all things that, in their humble way, these books shall be the ambassadors of good-will and understanding between East and West, the old world of Thought, and the new of Action. In this endeavour, and in their own sphere, they are but followers of the highest example in the land. They are confident that a deeper knowledge of the great ideals and lofty philosophy of Oriental thought may help to a revival of that true spirit of Charity which neither despises nor fears the nations of another creed and colour. Finally, in thanking press and public for the very cordial reception given to the "Wisdom of the East" series, they wish to state that no pains have been spared to secure the best specialists for the treatment of the various subjects at hand.

L. CRANMER-BYNG,
S. A. KAPADIA.

NORTHBROOK SOCIETY,
185 PICCADILLY, W.

THE
INSTRUCTION OF PTAH-HOTEP

—◆—

INTRODUCTION

Is there anything whereof it may be said,
  See, this is new?
It hath been already of old time,
  Which was before us.
There is no remembrance of former things;
  Neither shall there be any remembrance
Of things that are to come
  With those that shall come after.

IN these days, when all things and memories of the past are at length become not only subservient to, but submerged by, the matters and needs of the immediate present, those paths of knowledge that lead into regions seemingly remote from such needs are somewhat discredited; and the aims of those that follow them whither they lead are regarded as quite out of touch with the real interests of life. Very greatly is this so with archæology, and the study of ancient and curious tongues, and searchings into old thoughts on high and ever-insistent questions; a public which has hardly time to

read more than its daily newspaper and its
weekly novel has denounced—almost dismissed—
them, with many other noble and wonderful
things, as 'unpractical,' whatever that vague
and hollow word may mean.

As to those matters which lie very far back, concerning the lands of several thousand years ago, it
is very generally held that they are the proper and
peculiar province of specialists, dry-as-dusts, and
persons with an irreducible minimum of human
nature. It is thought that knowledge concerning
them, not the blank ignorance regarding them that
almost everywhere obtains, is a thing of which
to be rather ashamed, a detrimental possession ;
in a word, that the subject is not only unprofit-
able (a grave offence), but also uninteresting,
and therefore contemptible. This is a true
estimate of general opinion, although there are
those who will, for their own sakes, gainsay it.

When, therefore, I state that one of the writings
herein translated has an age of nearly six thousand years, and that another is but five hundred
years younger, it is likely that many will find
this sufficient reason against further perusal,
deeming it impossible that such things can possess
attraction for one not an enthusiast for them.
Yet so few are the voices across so great a span
of years that those among them having anything
to tell us should be welcome exceedingly ;
whereas, for the most part, they have cried in the

wilderness of neglect hitherto, or fallen on ears filled with the clamour of more instant things.

I could show, if this were a fitting place, that Archæology is not at all divorced from life, nor even devoid of emotion as subtle and strange, as swift and moving, as that experienced by those who love and follow Art. She, Archæology, is, for those who know her, full of such emotion; garbed in an imperishable glamour, she is raised far above the turmoil of the present on the wings of Imagination. Her eyes are sombre with the memory of the wisdom driven from her scattered sanctuaries; and at her lips wonderful things strive for utterance. In her are gathered together the longings and the laughter, the fears and failures, the sins and splendours and achievements of innumerable generations of men; and by her we are shown all the elemental and terrible passions of the unchanging soul of man, to which all cultures and philosophies are but garments to hide its nakedness; and thus in her, as in Art, some of us may realise ourselves. Withal she is heavy-hearted, making continual lamentation for a glory that has withered and old hopes without fulfilment; and all her habitations are laid waste.

As for the true lover of all old and forgotten things, it may justly be said of him, as of the poet, *Nascitur, non fit*. For the dreams and the wonder are with him from the beginning; and in early childhood, knowing as yet hardly

the names of ancient peoples, he is conscious
of, and yearns instinctively toward, an immense
and ever-receding past. With the one, as with
the other, the unaccountable passion is so knitted
into his soul that it will never, among a thousand
distractions and adverse influences, entirely for-
sake him; nor can such an one by willing cause
it to come or to depart. He will live much in
imagination, therein treading fair places now
enwrapped in their inevitable shroud of wind-
blown sand·; building anew temples whose
stones hardly remain one upon the other, con-
secrate to gods dead as their multitudes of
worshippers; holding converse with the sages
who, with all their lore, could not escape the
ultimate oblivion: a spectator of splendid
pageants, a ministrant at strange rites, a witness
to vast tragedies, he also has admittance to the
magical kingdom, to which is added the freedom
of the city of Remembrance. His care will be
to construct, patiently and with much labour,
a picture (which is often less than an outline)
of the conditions of the humanity that has been;
and he neither rejects nor despises any relic,
however trivial or unlovely, that will help him,
in its degree, to understand better that humanity
or to bridge the wide chasms of his ignorance.
Moreover, great age hallows all things, even
the most mean, investing them with a certain
sanctity; and the little sandal of a nameless

child, or the rude amulet placed long ago with weeping on the still bosom of a friend, will move his heart as strongly by its appeal as the proud and enduring monument of a great conqueror insatiable of praise. At times, moving among the tokens of a period that the ravenous years dare not wholly efface in passing, he hears, calling faintly as from afar, innumerable voices— the voices of those who, stretching forth in Sheol eager hands toward Life, greatly desire that some memorial of them, be it but a name, may survive in the world of men. . . .

Ancient Egypt fares perhaps better than other countries of antiquity at the hands of the ' general reader,' and sometimes obtains a hearing when they do not, by reason of its intimate contact at certain periods with the nation that has brought us the *Old Testament*. Because of this the report of it has been with us constantly, and it has nearly become a symbol in religion. The stories of Moses and the magicians, and of the dealings of Abraham and Joseph with Pharaoh, together with the rude woodcuts of Egyptian taskmasters and cupbearers in family Bibles, have invested the venerable land with a dreamy mystery; while every one has heard of ' Rameses, the Pharaoh of the Oppression,' and ' Meneptah, the Pharaoh of the Exodus.' And it is possible that for the sake of such association, if not for his own sake, Ptah-hotep will be considered worthy of notice.

But in spite of the fact that the Ancient Egyptians enjoy rather more popularity than their contemporaries, it is evident that the books which they wrote are closed books to those who have not the glamour of vanished peoples, and the fascination of mighty cities now made desolate, strong upon them.

Yet in the heterogeneous and pitiful flotsam that reluctant seas have washed to us piecemeal from a remote past, there are, as will be shown later, many things which, although proceeding from a culture and modes of thought as far removed from our own as they may well be,[1] are worth the reading, which do not require any special knowledge for their understanding; and of these are the translations in this book.

The following pages, which, although addressed to the 'general reader,' may yet be of some assistance to those especially interested in Egypt, give, among other matters, the place of the Instructions of Ptah-hotep and Ke'gemni in the 'literature' of Egypt; their place—their

---

[1] Much ingenuity has been expended to show that Egyptian manners and customs, books, and other things, were "much the same" as our own, as though the supposed similarity reflected any credit either on them or on us. Except in customs which are common to all times and places, as drinking beer, writing love-letters, making wills, going to school, and other things antecedently probable, the Egyptian life can show very few parallels to the life of to-day.

unique place—in the literature of the world ;
their value historically ; a description of the
document in which they were found ; what is
known of their authors ; a discussion of their
contents.

The land of which the Father of History
declared that no other country held so many
wonders, has bequeathed us, by various channels,
the rumour and remnant of a strange knowledge.   She has devised us enigmas insoluble,
and rendered up to us signs and messages whose
meaning is dark for all time.   And she has left
a religion, ' veiled in allegory and illustrated by
symbol,' as fascinating as impenetrable for those
who approach it.   For into our hands the keys of
these things have not been delivered ; wherefore
much study of them is a weariness to the flesh,
and of the hazarding of interpretations there is
no end.
But apart from the mazes of mythology, the
broken ways of history and the empty letter of a
dead faith, there are, as is known to some, and as
this little book professes to show, many documents
which are antique, but not antiquated, possessing
interest above the purely archæological—the
interest called human.   Of these are the tales
which recall, in incident as in style, those of the
immortal collection, full of the whole glamour
of the East, the *Thousand Nights and a Night.*

B

Such are the love-songs, full of the burning utterance of desire ; the pathetic and even bitter dirges, whose singers have seen all the works that are done under the sun, and found all to be vanity and vexation of spirit. And such also are the didactic poems for the instruction of youth, which—in poetic phrase and in great detail—inculcate, among other things, the practice of right conduct as the price of happiness ; a courtesy hardly less considerate than our own ; and a charity which, when certain inevitable shortcomings are allowed for, bears comparison with almost any later system.   Out of these there are many that may properly claim a place in a series bearing the seal of the Wisdom of the East, though they belong only to the more objective and ' practical ' side of that Wisdom.

But, as touching the books here translated— the Instructions of Ptah-hotep and of Ke'gemni— they possess, apart from the curious nature of their contents, a feature of the greatest interest, and an adequate claim on the notice of all persons interested in literature and its history.   For if the datings and ascriptions in them be accepted as trustworthy (there is no reason why they should not be so accepted), they were composed about four thousand years before Christ, and three thousand five hundred and fifty years before Christ, respectively.   And the significance of those remote dates is, that they are the oldest *books* in the world, the earliest extant specimens of the literary art. They stand on the extreme horizon of all that ocean of paper and ink that has become to us as an atmosphere, a fifth element, an essential of life.

Books of many kinds had of course been written for centuries before Ptah-hotep of Memphis summarised, for the benefit of future generations, the leading principles of morality current in his day; even before the Vizier, five hundred years earlier, gave to his children the scroll which they prized above all things on earth; [1] but those have perished and these remain. There are lists of titles which have a large sound, and prayers to the Gods for all good things, on the tombs and monuments of kings and magnates long before the time of Ke'gemni; but those are not books in any sense of that word. Even the long, strange chants and spells engraven in the Royal Pyramids over against Memphis are later than the time of Ptah-hotep, and cannot be called books in their present form, although some of them apparently originated before the First Dynasty. [2]

Nor do the oldest books of any other country approach these two in antiquity. To draw

[1] The monuments leave no doubt of this. Pen and ink were used in the First Dynasty, and speech had been reduced to visible signs before that.

[2] About B.C. 4770. In all Egyptian dates given in this book I follow Professor Petrie's chronology.

comparisons between them let us, in imagination, place ourselves at the period at which Ptah-hotep lived, that is, about B.C. 3550, 'under King Isôsi, living for ever,' and take a glance at futurity.

The Babylonians are doubtless exercising their literary talents; but they will leave nothing worthy the name of book to the far posterity of fifty-four centuries hence. Thirteen centuries shall pass before Hammurabi, King of Babylon, drafts the code of laws that will be found at that time. Only after two thousand years shall Moses write on the origin of things, and the Vedas be arranged in their present form. It will be two-and-a-half thousand years before the Great King of Jerusalem will set in order many proverbs and write books so much resembling, in form and style, that of Ptah-hotep;[1] before the source and summit of European literature will write his world epics. For the space of years between Solomon and ourselves, great though it seem, is not so great as that between Solomon and Ptah-hotep.

The number of extant texts of the class to which the subjoined immediately belong is not large in proportion to the rest of Egyptian MSS.,

[1] These are round figures, of course, and in the case of Solomon and Moses traditional dates. Modern criticism places *Genesis* and *Proverbs* much later than 1500 and 1000 B.C.

but they seem to be representative of the class, being diverse in date and subject, but similar in form. There is great uniformity in the arrangement of most of them, in the following respects. They have as title the word 'Instruction' (*seb'ôyet*), and are written by a father for the advantage of his son; they are very poetic in their arrangement of words and phrases, and are usually divided into short sections or paragraphs by the use of red ink for the first sentence of each. Such is the Instruction of Ptah-hotep on morality (the finest of its class); the Instruction of King Amenemhê'et on the hollowness of friendship and other matters; the Instruction of Deu'of, the son of Kherti, on the excellence of the literary life; and others. In many respects and in many details they greatly resemble the didactic works of the *Old Testament* and *Apocrypha*.

These 'Instructions' were held in high esteem as text-books and writing exercises in schools—a circumstance to which we owe the preservation of many of them. For a considerable number of important and interesting poems, letters, and narratives are only known to us from school exercise-books. The pupil at the 'Chamber of Instruction' wrote out about three pages of these each day, as a means of improving his writing, as a model of style in composition, and for purposes of edification. These exercises abound in errors of spelling and grammar, having sometimes the master's corrections elegantly written above in red. As may be imagined, a schoolboy's scrawl over three thousand years old is no easy thing to translate; but *faute de mieux* the Egyptologist welcomes any version, even the most barbarous. Fortunately, the MS. from which these translations come is not of this kind; a detailed description of it may interest some of my readers.

The Prisse Papyrus, which is well known by name and a few extracts to all persons conversant with Egyptian matters, was acquired in Egypt by M. Prisse d'Avennes, a French archæologist of distinction, and published by him in 1847.[1] The exact place of its discovery is unknown. M. Prisse is said to have bought it of one of the *fellahîn* whom he employed to make excavations at the burial-ground of Thebes. This man pretended that he had no knowledge of its finding, as he was trying to sell it for a friend. It is believed that it was actually taken by the Arab from the tomb of one of the Kings 'Entef;[2] but this is not certain. If it were, it would perhaps enable us to fix a *terminus ad quem* for the writing of this copy, although tombs often contain objects of later date. The papyrus was presented in about 1847, by M. Prisse, to the

[1] See Appendix for the literature of this papyrus.
[2] These were kings of the Eleventh Dynasty, about 2985 B.C.

Bibliothèque Nationale (in those days the Bibliothèque Royale) at Paris, where it still is, divided and glazed in the usual manner.

Spread out flat, it measures about 23 ft. 7 in., with an average height of 5⅞ in., which is about the usual height of papyri of the Eleventh and Twelfth Dynasties. It contains at present eighteen pages of heavy and bold black and red writing, in the so-called hieratic character. At first sight it appears to be in perfect preservation, being entirely free from the cracks and decay which mar many fine manuscripts of far later date; but an examination of the contents shows that an unknown quantity has been torn off from the commencement. Originally the roll contained at least two books, of which we have the latter part of one and the whole of the other. Between these there is a blank space of some 53 in.

The characters are clearly and carefully made, but are not always correct, as though the copyist had a badly written or very cursive copy before him, and was not always sure of his spelling.

The first of these books, of which only the last two pages remain to us, is a treatise on deportment, and is here called the *Instruction of Ke'gemni*. It has always been attributed to this person since its discovery, but examination of as much of the book as exists will show that it is not said to have been written by him. Because his is the only name mentioned, Egyptologists have concluded that he is the author. The unnamed Vizier, who called his children to him, can hardly be Ke'gemni, who was not raised to the rank of Vizier and Governor of a city until afterwards. Ke'gemni may well have been a son of the author. This is not of material importance, however, as the date of writing is given as the end of the reign of Heuni, the last King of the Third Dynasty, who died about 3998 B.C. This book, then, which argues a society of some refinement, is, so far as it goes, the oldest in the world.

After a long stretch of blank papyrus, from which a third book has perhaps been erased, we come upon the *Instruction of Ptah-hotep* in its entirety, divided into sections by red writing, as aforesaid.[1] In this, also, we get a definite date, for we learn in the opening lines that its author (or compiler) lived in the reign of King Isôsi. Now Isôsi was the last ruler but one of the Fifth Dynasty, and ruled forty-four years, from about 3580 to 3536 B.C. Thus we may take about 3550 as the period of Ptah-hotep.

Of these two kings there is hardly anything to say. Heuni is only known to us by mention of his name ; we have no record of any act of his.

---

[1] In the translation these divisions are indicated, for purposes of reference, by numbers and letters, which are not, of course, in the original. So also in the *Instruction of Amenemhê'ot* (Appendix).

Of Isôsi the only exploit that remains is this : that he sent his Treasurer, Be'wêrded, to Somaliland [1] to obtain for him a certain kind of dwarf ; this the Treasurer brought back, and received much reward therefor.   That is all that is left of the reigns of two kings, who ruled long, who perhaps ruled greatly and wisely, having just cause to hope that their fame and the report of their good deeds might never pass away. Such is the fate of kings.

The copy of these Instructions that we have, the only complete copy,[2] is far later than the later of these dates.   An examination of the writing shows that it is not earlier than the Eleventh Dynasty, and is probably of the Twelfth.[3]   More than this cannot be said ; where it was written, by whom, and when, are not stated, as they are in many cases.   The writing lacks the fine regularity of that of the professional scribes of the Twelfth Dynasty, and has many points of divergence therefrom ; but the papyrus is assigned by the best judges to this period. This gives it an antiquity of about four thousand five hundred years ; and it looks good to last as long again, if only it be not examined overmuch nor brought out into the light too often.

[1] Pwenet : the identification is not certain.

[2] Fragments of another are in the British Museum.

[3] It has been thought to be as late as the Seventeenth (about 1600 B.C.), but the balance of opinion favours the above-mentioned period.

It is as fresh and readable as in the year after
it was written. Will the books of our time last
one-tenth so long ? It is not without a feeling
of awe, even of sadness, that one with any sense
of the wonder of things gazes for the first time
on the old book, and thinks of all it has survived.
So many empires have arisen and gone down
since those words were penned, so many great
and terrible things have been.

And we are fortunate indeed in having such
a book as this of Ptah-hotep for the most ancient
complete literary work extant. For not by any
magical texts, or hymns and prayers, should we
be so well shown the conditions of that early
time ; but our moralist, by advancing counsels
of perfection for every contingency, has left us
a faithful record of his age. The veil of five-and-
a-half thousand years is rent, and we are met with
a vivid and a fascinating picture of the domestic
and social life of the ' Old Kingdóm.' We read
of the wife, who must be treated kindly at
all costs ; the genial generosity of the rich man,
and the scowling boor, a thorn in the side of his
friends and relations, the laughing-stock of all
men ; the unquenchable talkers of every station
in life, who argue high, who argue low, who
also argue round about them, as common as now
in the East, and the trusted councillor, weighing
every word ; the obstinate *ignoramus* who sees

everything inverted, listening open-mouthed to the disjointed gossip of those near him, and the scholar, conversing freely with learned and unlearned alike, recognising that, measured against the infinite possibilities of knowledge and skill, we are all much of the same stature; the master of the estate or province, treated with infinite respect by his subordinates in rank and wealth, and the paid servants that are never satisfied, who leave after presents have been made them; the hard-working clerk who casts accounts all day, and the tradesmen who will perhaps give you credit when money is dear, if you have previously made friends of them; the well-bred diner-out, lightly passing on his favourite dish, contenting himself with plain fare, and the *gourmand* who visits his friends at meal-times, departing only when the larder is entirely exhausted.

Not only do we find such characters as these in Ptah-hotep's hand-book, but interesting scenes are brought near to us by the writing-reed of that primæval Chesterfield. We find ourselves taking supper at the table of a great man. His subordinates sit round, scarcely daring to raise their eyes from their food, not speaking to their host until spoken to. He serves the food that is before him according to his liking for each guest; and the less favoured find solace in the reflection that even the distribution of food is

according to Providence. We pass on. Now we
are in the hall of council with the other overseers
and officials of the province, and our overlord
presiding. We notice with astonishment the
extreme solemnity and strict observance of
custom and precedence in this archaic period.
Many of those who have met report on the
matters under their charge, and others debate on
them. The one now speaking is discussing a
trade about which he knows nothing, and an
expert rises and makes very short work of his
opponent's arguments. Now we are among
some people dividing up property. One of them
has tried, of course, to bully his friends into giving
him more than his due share, and, having failed,
leaves the house in a rage. He will regret it
later. And so on.

Nothing definite is known concerning these
two nobles beyond what is said of them in their
works. A fine tomb of a certain Ke'gemni exists
at Memphis ; his titles, so far as can be ascer-
tained,[1] are : *Judge of the High Court : Governor
of the Land unto its Limit, South and North :
Director of every Command.* He has sometimes
been supposed to be identical with our Ke'gemni ;

[1] The inscriptions and sculptures from this tomb have not yet
been published, but a work dealing with it will shortly appear.
The above titles, excepting the first, are from Lepsius, *Denkmäler
aus Ägypten und Äthiopien*, Abth. II. 48, Berlin, 1849-58.

but I am assured by those most competent to judge that this tomb cannot be earlier than the Fifth Dynasty (a good three hundred years from the date assigned to the moralist), so that the theory that they are one person may be dismissed as highly improbable. No other person of the name is known.

The position is much the same with Ptah-hotep. There are near Memphis the tombs of several nobles of this name, of whom two lived in the reign of Isôsi ; and in this case, again, it has been assumed that one [1] of these two must be the writer of the Instruction. But in neither instance do the titles coincide with or include those assigned to him. The highest title which he bears, *Eldest Son of the King*, does not anywhere appear in these tombs. It is true that one of these contemporaries was *Hereditary Chief*; but we know that Ptah-hotep was a common name at this time, and in the absence of more certain proof it will be well to abstain from the identification of like names upon insufficient grounds. Thus it is only by the chance discovery of this

[1] Called Ptah-hotep I. by Egyptologists. For a description of his tomb, see Mariette, A., *Les Mastabas de l'Ancien Empire*, Paris, 1889, D. 62. For the other Ptah-hotep under Isôsi, see Quibell, J. E., and Griffith, F. L., *Egyptian Research Account ; The Ramesseum and the Tomb of Ptah-hetep*, London, 1898. Also Davies, N. de G., and Griffith, F. L., *Egypt Exploration Fund ; The Mastaba of Ptahhetep and Akhethetep at Šaqqareh*, 2 vols., London, 1900, 1901. The little figure on the cover of this book is from this tomb.

scroll that these two princes of old time, whose
bodies are blown about the desert dust these
many centuries, are secured from utter oblivion ;
men ' *such as did bear rule in their kingdoms,
men renowned for their power, giving counsel by
their understanding, and declaring prophecies :
Leaders of the people by their counsels, and by
their knowledge of learning meet for the people,
wise and eloquent in their instructions.*' And
against such as these, that from remote years
' *have left a name behind them, that their praises
might be reported,*' how many are there ' *which
have no memorial ; who are perished, as though
they had never been ; and are become as though
they had never been born ; and their children after
them.*' [1]

I had intended to make a detailed analysis of
the moral sense of Ptah-hotep and Ke'gemni,
but it appears unnecessary ; since they give
their advice so clearly and simply, they may
safely be left to speak for themselves. But
as especially noteworthy I would point to the
gracious tolerance of ignorance enjoined in § 1
(Ptah-hotep), and the fine reason given for that
injunction, in contrast with the scorn expressed
for the obstinate fool (Ph. 40) ; the care due to
a wife (Ph. 21), which is in signal contrast to
the custom of other Eastern nations in this

[1] *The Wisdom of the Son of Sirach*, chap. xliv.

respect;[1] the great stress laid on filial duties
(Ph. 38, 39, 41, 42, 43); the enthusiasm for
obedience, expressed in a jargon of puns (Ph. 38),
which, once the high-watermark of style among
Egyptian *literati*, has long since lost its savour;
the interesting matter on manners at table
(Kg. 2, 3, Ph. 7, 9), in society (Kg. 4, Ph. 14, 18, 20,
34), and in official positions (Ph. 5, 8, 13, 15, 16,
17, 24, 28). A rough classification including
many sections is here given :

Duties toward superiors (Ph. 2, 7, 8, 10,
15, 27, 31).

Duties toward equals (3, 6, 14, 18, 20, 26, 29,
33, 35, 37).

Duties toward inferiors (1, 4, 5, 16, 17, 22).

The whole teaching resolves into the maxim,
" Be good, and you will be happy; " not at all
in the sense that virtue is its own reward—I do
not think that that would have seemed an
adequate return to Ptah-hotep—but in the sense
of material welfare rewarding, as a matter of
course, an honourable life. Following his reason-
ing, if a man be obedient as a son, punctilious
as a servant, generous and gentle as a master,
and courteous as a friend, then all good things
shall fall to him, he shall reach a green old age
honoured by the King, and his memory shall
be long in the land. This theory, which is not

---

[1] The Egyptians were monogamists at this time, and the wife
enjoyed social equality with her husband.

found satisfactory in our day, is insisted on by most of the ancient moralists, who appear to regard it, not as a substitute for conscience, but rather as a *raison d'être* or justification thereof. Yet, centuries before a King of Israel had seen all things that are, and found them vanity, a King of Egypt had left it on record that he had done all good things for his subjects, and that 'there was no satisfaction therein.'

It has been said with some truth of codes of morals and laws that what is omitted is almost as important as what is included. But we must not carry this too far; we should be foolish indeed did we assert that those things omitted from such a code as Ptah-hotep's were not practised or not held to be important in his day. For example, he 'knows nothing'—as a Higher Critic would say—of kindness to animals; but we know from many things that the Egyptians treated animals kindly and made much of them as pets. In the very tomb of that Ptah-hotep mentioned above,[1] who may be our author, is depicted the bringing of three dogs and a tame monkey to him while he is dressing; possibly so that he may feed them himself. And this kindly feeling obtained throughout Egyptian history. They treated animals more as 'dumb friends' in those days than might have been

[1] Page 29, footnote.

a priori expected, and more, perhaps, than any other nation of antiquity. Again, he 'knows nothing' of duties to the mother, although he is so insistent on duties to the father; but the high position of women and their matriarchal privileges oppose any deduction that Egyptian manners were somewhat to seek in this direction. Ke'gemni says of the unsociable man that he is a grief to his mother, and another moralist of uncertain date (perhaps Twelfth Dynasty, about B.C. 2700), named 'Eney, is explicit on this matter. He says to his son, '*I gave thee thy mother, she that bore thee with much suffering. . . . She placed thee at the Chamber of Instruction for the sake of thine instruction in books; she was constant to thee daily, having loaves and beer in her house. When thou art grown, and hast taken to thee a wife, being master in thy house, cast thine eyes on the one that gave thee birth and provided thee with all good things, as did thy mother. Let her not reproach thee, lest she lift up her hands to the God, and He hear her prayer.*'

And, most remarkable of all omissions, there is nothing said as to duties to the Gods. In Egypt, whose Gods are beyond counting, where almost everybody was a priest, Ptah-hotep—himself a 'Holy Father' and 'Beloved of the God'—has no word to say on religious obligations, devoting his work entirely to the principles of charity and duty to one's neighbour. It is seemingly sufficient to him that one do the right in this world, without thinking overmuch about the other. This is the more curious in that other writers of the same class have many injunctions regarding worship and sacrifice ; and so complete is his reserve touching this matter, so important in the eyes of other Egyptians, that it is easy to believe that it was intentional. We may even discern in him a protagonist of the modern ' Ethical School,' whose adherents may be interested to find their views implicitly held so long ago.

Notwithstanding this singularity, he is by no means unmindful of Deity. We notice that he has occasion to speak several times of ' the God ' [1] in His relation to humanity and human affairs. If we collect these references to the God, we shall find that the following qualities are attributed to Him. He rewards diligence (9, 10) and punishes sin (6, 10 ; also Kg. 5) ; He is the giver of good things (Ph. 22, 30, 43), dispenses fate and preordains events (6, 7, 9, 26), loves His creation (26), observes men's actions (10), desires them to be fruitful and multiply (12). All this is in complete accord with the belief of other religions—including Christianity—regarding the Godhead. And here we touch another pleasing characteristic of this most ancient of books—its catholic spirit and disregard of those

[1] *Nôter.*

mythological and esoteric riddles that most Egyptian works propound to us continually. It will be noticed that 'the God' is not anywhere mentioned by name. Osiris (5) and Horus (41) are alluded to, but only historically, in respect of their rule upon earth, not as present powers. The reason is this, that at that time the Gods, even the great Gods, were only local, that is to say, their worship was confined to certain towns or districts ('nomes'), and beyond the boundaries of these their names lost that power and influence which they exerted in their peculiar provinces. A book, therefore, which spoke of one God only—by name—would have been found much limited as to popularity and use. Hence the old moralists and didactic writers, whatever God they might themselves worship, forebore to mention Him, since by many readers He would not be recognised as paramount ; they wrote instead, 'The God,' that is, 'the God of your allegiance, whoever He may be.' Thus, were the reader a native of Heliopolis, his God would be Atômu, the Setting Sun ; of Memphis, Ptah, the Revealer ; of Hermopolis, Thoth, Master of Divine Words and Chief of the Eight. It was for this reason that the unknown author of what is called the 'Negative Confession'[1] makes the deceased say, '*I have not scorned the*

---

[1] This is an arbitrary name not existing in the original. It would be better named 'The Declaration of Innocence.'

God of my town.' And, indeed, so simply and
purely does Ptah-hotep speak of the God that
the modern reader can, without the least de-
gradation of his ideals, consider the author as
referring to the Deity of monotheism, and if he
be of Christendom, read God ; if of Islam, read
Allah ; if of Jewry, Jehovah.[1]

No doubt the gulf fixed between teaching and
practice was as great then as now. We have
the teaching, we know that the teaching was
current all over Egypt in various forms, but of
the practice we know very little.   Human nature
being much the same at all times and places, we
must beware of measuring the one by the other,
the unknown by the known, and must be content
to take such counsels as showing the Egyptian—

Not what he was, but what he should have been.

It is established that they were a kindly,
peace-loving people, genial and courtly ; but
whether law-abiding is another matter. We
know nothing about their laws, but we know

---

[1] It has been thought by many Egyptologists that ' the God '
mentioned in this and other texts is a nameless monotheistic
abstraction transcending all named gods. Although this theory
has the support of many great names, I venture to say that the
evidence for such an important doctrine is in the highest degree
unsatisfactory.

that the law-courts were busy, and that legal officials were numerous ; and we know, further, that their duplicity and lack of straightforwardness were proverbial among the Greeks and Romans, and persists to this day.

I have noted above the resemblance of the Egyptian Instructions to the Jewish didactic books (*Proverbs* and *Ecclesiastes* in the *Old Testament, Wisdom of Solomon* and *Ecclesiasticus* in the *Apocrypha*) ; this will be obvious to all readers. Compare, *e.g.*, the opening of Ptah-hotep (§B) with the opening of *Proverbs*. It is not necessary to point out all the parallels in detail.

I come, lastly, to speak of other translations.[1] The first into any language was that of the Rev. D. I. Heath, Vicar of Brading, Isle of Wight. This version, which first appeared in 1856, was ruined by the translator's theory that the Prisse Papyrus contained references to the Exodus, and was written by the ' Shepherd-King,' Aphobis. How he obtained that name from Ptah-hotep, how he read the Exodus into his book, or how he got three-fourths of his translation, it is not possible to say. Written in a style which is in itself a matter for decipherment, it is full of absurdities and gratuitous mistakes, and

[1] The books mentioned here are set forth in detail in the Bibliography.

is entirely worthless. It is one more instance of
the lamentable results that arise when a person
with a preconceived Biblical theory comes into
contact with Egyptian records. In the following
year M. Chabas did part of the papyrus into
French, and, as might be expected of an Egyptologist of such attainments, his version was
infinitely more accurate than the foregoing. In
1869 Herr Lauth made a translation—also
partial—into Latin, and in 1884 M. Philippe
Virey published a careful study and complete
translation of both books. His rendering [1] was
subsequently translated into English and published (with some alterations) in *Records of the
Past*, 1890, and has remained the only complete
translation in English. It has been taken bodily
(even the footnotes) into Myer's *Oldest Books in
the World*, and has been put into charming verse
by Canon Rawnsley in his *Notes for the Nile*.
Thus it appears to be, in a sense, the standard
version. Nevertheless, it leaves very much to be
desired in point of accuracy, although the general
sense of each section is usually caught. Of later
years Mr. Griffith has done important work on
this text, and I am indebted to his translations
for several readings.

As regards the version here offered, I will only
say that it has been done with considerable care,

[1] Only of Ptah-hotep.

without prejudice, and, it is thought, in accordance
with scientific methods of translation ; and that
it has been compared with all previous renderings,
and will be found to be, on the whole, the most
accurate that has yet appeared.

And now I will leave Ptah-hotep to speak for
himself. It may be thought that he has been
introduced at too great length ; but I would point
out that his book has been strangely overlooked
by the educated public hitherto, although it would
be difficult to over-estimate its importance, to
literature as the oldest complete book known,
to ethics and theology as the earliest expression
of the mystery we name Conscience, and to lovers
of antiquity as one of the most instructive and
touching relics of a people and a power that once
were great and are now brought to nothing. By
a happy chance the words of our sage have been
justified, in that he said, ' *No word that hath
here been set down shall cease out of the land for
ever.*' Would indeed that we had more of such
books as this, whereby we may a little lighten
the darkness that lies behind the risings of a
million suns ; and learn how little the human
heart, and the elements of human intercourse,
alter throughout the ages. And what of the
other writers of that time, whose works and
whose very names are entirely swept away ? To
this there is no better answer made than in the
lamentation made by the harper close upon five

thousand years ago, which was written up in the tomb of King 'Entef :

Those that built them tombs, he sang, *have now no resting-place. Lo ! what of their deeds ? I have heard the words of Yemhotep and of Hardedef, whose sayings men repeat continually. Behold ! where are their abodes ? Their walls are over-thrown, and their places are not, even as though they had not been.*'

The burden of Egypt.

BATTISCOMBE G. GUNN.

3, PARK HILL ROAD,
　CROYDON.

THE INSTRUCTION OF PTAH-HOTEP

THE Instruction of the Governor of his City, the Vizier, Ptah-hotep, in the Reign of the King of Upper and Lower Egypt, Isôsi, living for ever, to the end of Time.

A. The Governor of his City, the Vizier, Ptah-hotep, he said : ' O Prince, my Lord, the end of life is at hand ; old age descendeth [upon me] ; feebleness cometh, and childishness is renewed. He [that is old] lieth down in misery every day. The eyes are small ; the ears are deaf. Energy is diminished, the heart hath no rest. The mouth is silent, and he speaketh no word ; the heart stoppeth, and he remembereth not yesterday. The bones are painful throughout the body ; good turneth unto evil. All taste departeth. These things doeth old age for mankind, being evil in all things. The nose is stopped, and he breatheth not for weakness (?), whether standing or sitting.

' Command me, thy servant, therefore, to make over my princely authority [to my son]. Let me speak unto him the words of them that hearken to the counsel of the men of old time ; those that

41

hearkened unto the gods. I pray thee, let this thing be done, that sin may be banished from among persons of understanding, that thou may enlighten the lands.'

Said the Majesty of this God : [1] 'Instruct him, then, in the words of old time ; may he be a wonder unto the children of princes, that they may enter and hearken with him. Make straight all their hearts ; and discourse with him, without causing weariness.'

B. Here begin the proverbs of fair speech, spoken by the Hereditary Chief, the Holy Father,[2] Beloved of the God, the Eldest Son of the King, of his body, the Governor of his City, the Vezier, Ptah-hotep, when instructing the ignorant in the knowledge of exactness in fair-speaking ; the glory of him that obeyeth, the shame of him that transgresseth them.

He said unto his son :

1. Be not proud because thou art learned ; but discourse with the ignorant man, as with the sage. For no limit can be set to skill, neither is there any craftsman that possesseth full advantages. Fair speech is more rare than the emerald that is found by slave-maidens on the pebbles.

2. If thou find an arguer talking, one that is well disposed and wiser than thou, let thine arms

---

[1] The King.   [2] Title of an order of the priesthood.

fall, bend thy back,[1] be not angry with him if he agree (?) not with thee.   Refrain from speaking evilly ; oppose him not at any time when he speaketh. If he address thee as one ignorant of the matter, thine humbleness shall bear away his contentions.

3. If thou find an arguer talking, thy fellow, one that is within thy reach, keep not silence when he saith aught that is evil ; so shalt thou be wiser than he. Great will be the applause on the part of the listeners, and thy name shall be good in the knowledge of princes.

4. If thou find an arguer talking, a poor man, that is to say not thine equal, be not scornful toward him because he is lowly.   Let him alone ; then shall he confound himself. Question him not to please thine heart, neither pour out thy wrath upon him that is before thee ; it is shameful to confuse a mean mind. If thou be about to do that which is in thine heart, overcome it as a thing rejected of princes.

5. If thou be a leader, as one directing the conduct of the multitude, endeavour always to be gracious, that thine own conduct be without defect. Great is Truth, appointing a straight path ; never hath it been overthrown since the

---

[1] The customary attitude of a submissive inferior at that time.

reign of Osiris.[1] One that oversteppeth the laws shall be punished. Overstepping is by the covetous man ; but degradations (?) bear off his riches, for the season of his evil-doing ceaseth not. For he saith, ' I will obtain by myself for myself,' and saith not, ' I will obtain because I am allowed.' But the limits of justice are steadfast ; it is that which a man repeateth from his father.

6. Cause not fear among men ; for [this] the God punisheth likewise. For there is a man that saith, ' Therein is life ' ; and he is bereft of the bread of his mouth. There is a man that saith, ' Power [is therein] ' ; and he saith, ' I seize for myself that which I perceive.' Thus a man speaketh, and he is smitten down. It is another that attaineth by giving unto him that hath not ; not he that causeth men dread. For it happeneth that what the God hath commanded, even that thing cometh to pass. Live, therefore, in the house of kindliness, and men shall come and give gifts of themselves.

7. If thou be among the guests of a man that is greater than thou, accept that which he giveth thee, putting it to thy lips. If thou look at him that is before thee (thine host), pierce him not

[1] The God Osiris was believed to have reigned on earth many thousand years before Mênês, the first historical king.

with many glances. It is abhorred of the soul [1] to stare at him. Speak not till he address thee ; one knoweth not what may be evil in his opinion. Speak when he questioneth thee ; so shall thy speech be good in his opinion. The noble who sitteth before food divideth it as his soul moveth him ; he giveth unto him that he would favour— it is the custom of the evening meal. It is his soul that guideth his hand. It is the noble that bestoweth, not the underling that attaineth. Thus the eating of bread is under the providence of the God ; he is an ignorant man that disputeth it.

8. If thou be an emissary sent from one noble to another, be exact after the manner of him that sent thee, give his message even as he hath said it. Beware of making enmity by thy words, setting one noble against the other by perverting truth. Overstep it not, neither repeat that which any man, be he prince or peasant, saith in opening the heart ; it is abhorrent to the soul.

9. If thou have ploughed, gather thine harvest in the field, and the God shall make it great under thine hand. Fill not thy mouth at thy neighbours' table. . . .[2] If a crafty man be the

[1] Soul = *ka'*, and throughout this work. *Ka'* is translated *person* in § 22, *will* in § 27.
[2] An obscure or corrupt phrase here follows, which does not admit of satisfactory translation.

possessor of wealth, he stealeth like a crocodile from the priests.

Let not a man be envious that hath no children; let him be neither downcast nor quarrelsome on account of it. For a father, though great, may be grieved; as to the mother of children, she hath less peace than another. Verily, each man is created [to his destiny] by the God, Who is the chief of a tribe, trustful in following him.

10. If thou be lowly, serve a wise man, that all thine actions may be good before the God. If thou have known a man of none account that hath been advanced in rank, be not haughty toward him on account of that which thou knowest concerning him; but honour him that hath been advanced, according to that which he hath become.

Behold, riches come not of themselves; it is their rule for him that desireth them. If he bestir him and collect them himself, the God shall make him prosperous; but He shall punish him, if he be slothful.

11. Follow thine heart during thy lifetime; do not more than is commanded thee. Diminish not the time of following the heart; it is abhorred of the soul, that its time [of ease] be taken away. Shorten not the daytime more than is needful to

maintain thine house. When riches are gained,
follow the heart; for riches are of no avail if
one be weary.

12. If thou wouldest be a wise man, beget a
son for the pleasing of the God. If he make
straight his course after thine example, if he
arrange thine affairs in due order, do unto him
all that is good, for thy son is he, begotten of
thine own soul. Sunder not thine heart from
him, or thine own begotten shall curse [thee].
If he be heedless and trespass thy rules of
conduct, and is violent; if every speech that
cometh from his mouth be a vile word; then
beat thou him, that his talk may be fitting.
Keep him from those that make light of that
which is commanded, for it is they that make
him rebellious.[1] And they that are guided go
not astray, but they that lose their bearings
cannot find a straight course.

13. If thou be in the chamber of council, act
always according to the steps enjoined on thee
at the beginning of the day. Be not absent, or
thou shalt be expelled; but be ready in entering
and making report. Wide [2] is the seat of one
that hath made address. The council-chamber
acteth by strict rule; and all its plans are in
accordance with method. It is the God that

[1] Translation doubtful.   [2] *i.e.* comfortable.

advanceth one to a seat therein ; the like is not done for elbowers.

14. If thou be among people, make for thyself love, the beginning and end of the heart. One that knoweth not his course shall say in himself (seeing thee), 'He that ordereth himself duly becometh the owner of wealth ; I shall copy his conduct.' Thy name shall be good, though thou speak not ; thy body shall be fed ; thy face shall be [seen] among thy neighbours ; thou shalt be provided with what thou lackest. As to the man whose heart obeyeth his belly, he causeth disgust in place of love. His heart is wretched (?), his body is gross (?), he is insolent toward those endowed of the God. He that obeyeth his belly hath an enemy.[1]

15. Report thine actions without concealment ; discover thy conduct when in council with thine overlord. It is not evil for the envoy that his report be not answered, 'Yea, I know it,' by the prince ; for that which he knoweth includeth not [this]. If he (the prince) think that he will oppose him on account of it, [he thinketh] 'He will be silent because I have spoken.'[2]

16. If thou be a leader, cause that the rules

[1] His belly, presumably.
[2] The above translation is not satisfactory ; the text may be corrupt. No intelligible translation of it has yet been made.

that thou hast enjoined be carried out ; and do all things as one that remembereth the days coming after, when speech availeth not. Be not lavish of favours ; it leadeth to servility (?), producing slackness.

17. If thou be a leader, be gracious when thou hearkenest unto the speech of a suppliant. Let him not hesitate to deliver himself of that which he hath thought to tell thee ; but be desirous of removing his injury. Let him speak freely, that the thing for which he hath come to thee may be done. If he hesitate to open his heart, it is said, ' Is it because he (the judge) doeth the wrong that no entreaties are made to him concerning it by those to whom it happeneth ? ' But a well-taught heart hearkeneth readily.

18. If thou desire to continue friendship in any abode wherein thou enterest, be it as master, as brother, or as friend ; wheresoever thou goest, beware of consorting with women. No place prospereth wherein that is done. Nor is it prudent to take part in it ; a thousand men have been ruined for the pleasure of a little time short as a dream. Even death is reached thereby ; it is a wretched thing. As for the evil liver, one leaveth him for what he doeth, he is avoided. If his desires be not gratified, he regardeth (?) no laws.

D

19. If thou desire that thine actions may be good, save thyself from all malice, and beware of the quality of covetousness, which is a grievous inner (?) malady. Let it not chance that thou fall thereinto. It setteth at variance fathers-in-law and the kinsmen of the daughter-in-law ; it sundereth the wife and the husband. It gathereth unto itself all evils ; it is the girdle of all wickedness.[1] But the man that is just flourisheth ; truth goeth in his footsteps, and he maketh habitations therein, not in the dwelling of covetousness.

20. Be not covetous as touching shares, in seizing that which is not thine own property. Be not covetous toward thy neighbours ; for with a gentle man praise availeth more than might. He [that is covetous] cometh empty from among his neighbours, being void of the persuasion of speech. One hath remorse for even a little covetousness when his belly cooleth.

21. If thou wouldest be wise, provide for thine house, and love thy wife that is in thine arms. Fill her stomach, clothe her back ; oil is the remedy of her limbs. Gladden her heart during thy lifetime, for she is an estate profitable unto its lord. Be not harsh, for gentleness mastereth her more than strength. Give (?) to her that for which she sigheth and that toward which her

_____
[1] *i.e.* all wickedness is contained therein.

eye looketh; so shalt thou keep her in thine house. . . .

22. Satisfy thine hired servants out of such things as thou hast; it is the duty of one that hath been favoured of the God. In sooth, it is hard to satisfy hired servants. For one[1] saith, ' He is a lavish person; one knoweth not that which may come [from him].' But on the morrow he thinketh, ' He is a person of exactitude (parsimony), content therein.' And when favours have been shown unto servants, they say, ' We go.' Peace dwelleth not in that town wherein dwell servants that are wretched.

23. Repeat not extravagant speech, neither listen thereto; for it is the utterance of a body heated by wrath. When such speech is repeated to thee, hearken not thereto, look to the ground. Speak not regarding it, that he that is before thee may know wisdom. If thou be commanded to do a theft, bring it to pass that the command be taken off thee, for it is a thing hateful according to law. That which destroyeth a vision is the veil over it.

24. If thou wouldest be a wise man, and one sitting in council with his overlord, apply thine heart unto perfection. Silence is more profitable unto thee than abundance of speech. Consider

---

[1] A servant.

how thou may be opposed by an expert that speaketh in council. It is a foolish thing to speak on every kind of work, for he that disputeth thy words shall put them unto proof.

25. If thou be powerful, make thyself to be honoured for knowledge and for gentleness. Speak with authority, that is, not as if following injunctions, for he that is humble (when highly placed) falleth into errors. Exalt not thine heart, that it be not brought low.[1] Be not silent, but beware of interruption and of answering words with heat. Put it far from thee; control thyself. The wrathful heart speaketh fiery words; it darteth out at the man of peace that approacheth, stopping his path.

One that reckoneth accounts all the day passeth not an happy moment. One that gladdeneth his heart all the day provideth not for his house. The bowman hitteth the mark, as the steersman reacheth land, by diversity of aim. He that obeyeth his heart shall command.[2]

26. Let not a prince be hindered when he is occupied; neither oppress the heart of him that is already laden. For he shall be hostile toward one that delayeth him, but shall bare his soul

[1] Compare Prov. xvii. 18.
[2] So also in life, by diversity of aim, alternating work and play, happiness is secured. Tacking is evidently meant in the case of the steersman.

unto one that loveth him. The disposal of souls is with the God, and that which He loveth is His creation. Set out, therefore, after a violent quarrel ; be at peace with him that is hostile unto [thee] his opponent. It is such souls that make love to grow.

27. Instruct a noble in such things as be profitable unto him ; cause that he be received among men. Let his satisfaction fall on his master, for thy provision dependeth upon his will. By reason of it thy belly shall be satisfied ; thy back will be clothed thereby. Let him receive thine heart, that thine house may flourish and thine honour—if thou wish it to flourish—thereby. He shall extend thee a kindly hand. Further, he shall implant the love of thee in the bodies of thy friends. Forsooth, it is a soul loving to hearken.[1]

28. If thou be the son of a man of the priesthood, and an envoy to conciliate the multitude, ...[2] speak thou without favouring one side. Let it not be said, 'His conduct is that of the nobles, favouring one side in his speech.' Turn thine aim toward exact judgments.

[1] This section refers to the relations between the son of a nobleman and his tutor, dwelling on the benefits from former pupils in high places, if their schooldays have been pleasant. The last sentence of this section, as of sections 23 and 25, is somewhat *à propos des bottes*.

[2] An obscure phrase is here.

29. If thou have been gracious at a former time, having forgiven a man to guide him aright, shun him, remind him not after the first day that he hath been silent to thee [concerning it].

30. If thou be great, after being of none account, and hast gotten riches after squalor, being foremost in these in the city, and hast knowledge concerning useful matters, so that promotion is come unto thee; then swathe not thine heart in thine hoard, for thou art become the steward of the endowments of the God. Thou art not the last; another shall be thine equal, and to him shall come the like [fortune and station].

31. Bend thy back unto thy chief, thine overseer in the King's palace, for thine house dependeth upon his wealth, and thy wages in their season. How foolish is one that quarrelleth with his chief, for one liveth only while he is gracious. . . .
Plunder not the houses of tenants; neither steal the things of a friend, lest he accuse thee in thine hearing, which thrusteth back the heart.[1] If he know of it, he will do thee an injury. Quarrelling in place of friendship is a foolish thing.

[1] Literally, "It is that which preventeth the heart from advancing (?)" A curious phrase.

32. [Concerning continence].

33. If thou wouldest seek out the nature of
a friend, ask it not of any companion of his ; but
pass a time with him alone, that thou injure not
his affairs.   Debate with him after a season ; test
his heart in an occasion of speech.   When he
hath told thee his past life, he hath made an
opportunity that thou may either be ashamed
for him or be familiar with him.   Be not reserved
with him when he openeth speech, neither answer
him after a scornful manner.   Withdraw not
thyself from   him,   neither   interrupt (?)   him
whose matter is not yet ended, whom it is possible
to benefit.

34. Let thy face be bright what time thou
livest.   That which goeth into the storehouse
must come out therefrom ; and bread is to be
shared.   He that is grasping in entertainment shall
himself have an empty belly ; he that causeth
strife cometh himself to sorrow.   Take not such
an one for thy companion.   It is a man's kindly
acts that are remembered of him in the years after
his life.[1]

35. Know well thy merchants ; for when thine
affairs are in evil case, thy good repute among
thy friends is a channel (?) which is filled.   It is
more important than the dignities of a man ; and

[1] Literally, after his stick or sceptre.

the wealth of one passeth to another. The good repute of a man's son is a glory unto him ; and a good character is for remembrance.

36. Correct chiefly ; instruct conformably [therewith]. Vice must be drawn out, that virtue may remain. Nor is this a matter of misfortune, for one that is a gainsayer becometh a strife-maker.

37. If thou make a woman to be ashamed, wanton of heart, one known by her townsfolk to be falsely placed, be kind unto her for a space, send her not away, give her to eat. The wanton-ness of her heart shall esteem thy guidance.

c. If thou obey these things that I have said unto thee, all thy demeanour shall be of the best ; for, verily, the quality of truth is among their excellences. Set the memory of them in the mouths of the people ; for their proverbs are good. Nor shall any word that hath here been set down cease out of this land for ever, but shall be made a pattern whereby princes shall speak well. They (my words) shall instruct a man how he shall speak, after he hath heard them ; yea, he shall become as one skilful in obeying, excellent in speaking, after he hath heard them. Good fortune shall befall him, for he shall be of the highest rank. He shall be gracious to the end of his life ; he shall be con-

tented always. His knowledge shall be his
guide (?) into a place of security, wherein he
shall prosper while on earth. The scholar [1] shall
be content in his knowledge. As to the prince,
in his turn, forsooth, his heart shall be happy,
his tongue made straight. And [in these pro-
verbs] his lips shall speak, his eyes shall see, and
his ears shall hear, that which is profitable for
his son, so that he deal justly, void of deceit.

38. A splendid thing is the obedience of
an obedient son; he cometh in and listeneth
obediently.

Excellent in hearing, excellent in speaking, is
every man that obeyeth what is noble; and the
obedience of an obeyer is a noble thing.

Obedience is better than all things that are;
it maketh good-will.

How good it is that a son should take that
from his father by which he hath reached old
age (Obedience).

That which is desired by the God is obedience;
disobedience is abhorred of the God.

Verily, it is the heart that maketh its master
to obey or to disobey; for the safe and sound
life of a man are his heart.

It is the obedient man that obeyeth what is
said; he that loveth to obey, the same shall carry
out commands.

[1] Who knows them.

He that obeyeth becometh one obeyed.

It is good indeed when a son obeyeth his father ; and he (his father) that hath spoken hath great joy of it. Such a son shall be mild as a master, and he that heareth him shall obey him that hath spoken. He shall be comely in body and honoured by his father. His memory shall be in the mouths of the living, those upon earth, as long as they exist.[1]

39. Let a son receive the word of his father, not being heedless of any rule of his. Instruct thy son [thus] ; for the obedient man is one that is perfect in the opinion of princes. If he direct his mouth by what hath been enjoined him, watchful and obedient, thy son shall be wise, and his goings seemly. Heedlessness leadeth unto disobedience on the morrow ; but understanding shall stablish him. As for the fool, he shall be crushed.

40. As for the fool, devoid of obedience, he doeth nothing. Knowledge he regardeth as ignorance, profitable things as hurtful things. He doeth all kind of errors, so that he is rebuked therefor every day. He liveth in death there-

---

[1] The greater part of this section is a play upon the root *sôdem*, which in its meaning includes our *hear* (*listen*) and *obey*. This tiresome torture of words is frequent in Egyptian, especially in old religious texts.

with ; it is his food. At chattering speech he marvelleth, as at the wisdom of princes, living in death every day. He is shunned because of his misfortunes, by reason of the multitude of afflictions that cometh upon him every day.

41. A son that hearkeneth is as a Follower of Horus.[1] He is good after he hearkeneth ; he groweth old, he reacheth honour and reverence. He repeateth in like manner to his sons and daughters, so renewing the instruction of his father. Each man instructeth as did his begetter, repeating it unto his children. Let them [in turn] speak with their sons and daughters, that they may be famous in their deeds. Let that which thou speakest implant true things and just in the life of thy children. Then the highest authority shall arrive, and sins depart [from them]. And such men as see these things shall say, 'Surely that man hath spoken to good purpose,' and they shall do likewise ; or, 'But surely that man was experienced.' And all people shall declare, 'It is they that shall direct the multitude ; dignities are not complete without them.'

Take not any word away, neither add one ;

[1] The "Followers of Horus" are a legendary dynasty of demigods, believed by the Egyptians to have ruled for about 13,400 years after the reign of Horus, and before that of Mênês. There is also an order of spirits of this name.

set not one in the place of another. Beware of opening . . .[1] in thyself.

Be wary of speech when a learned man hearkeneth unto thee ; desire to be stablished for good in the mouth of those that hear thee speaking. If thou have entered as an expert, speak with exact (?) lips, that thy conduct may be seemly.

42. Be thine heart overflowing ; but refrain thy mouth. Let thy conduct be exact while amongst nobles, and seemly before thy lord, doing that which he hath commanded. Such a son shall speak unto them that hearken to him ; moreover, his begetter shall be favoured. Apply thine heart, what time thou speakest, to saying things such that the nobles who listen declare, 'How excellent is that which cometh out of his mouth !'

43. Carry out the behest of thy lord to thee. How good is the teaching of a man's father, for he hath come from him, who hath spoken of his son while he was yet unborn ; and that which is done for him (the son) is more than that which is commanded him. Forsooth, a good son is of the gift of the God ; he doeth more than is

[1] A word of unknown meaning ; apparently some kind of plant. Such a word seems out of place here, and may be idiomatic, like our "flowery language." But the preceding line obviously refers to this book.

enjoined on him, he doeth right, and putteth his heart into all his goings.

D. If now thou attain my position, thy body shall flourish, the King shall be content in all that thou doest, and thou shalt gather years of life not fewer than I have passed upon earth. I have gathered even fivescore and ten years of life, for the King hath bestowed upon me favours more than upon my forefathers; this because I wrought truth and justice for the King unto mine old age.

IT IS FINISHED
FROM ITS BEGINNING TO ITS END
EVEN AS FOUND IN WRITING.

THE INSTRUCTION OF KE'GEMNI

1.[1] The cautious man flourisheth, the exact one is praised ; the innermost chamber openeth unto the man of silence. Wide [2] is the seat of the man gentle of speech ; but knives are prepared against one that forceth a path, that he advance not, save in due season.

2. If thou sit with a company of people, desire not the bread that thou likest : short is the time of restraining the heart, and gluttony is an abomination ; therein is the quality of a beast. A cup of water quencheth the thirst, and a mouthful of melon supporteth the heart. A good thing standeth for goodness, but some small thing standeth for plenty.[3] A base man is he that is governed by his belly ; he departeth only when he is no longer able to fill full his belly in men's houses.

[1] The original is not divided into sections.
[2] *i.e.* comfortable
[3] This is a rather dark saying, but apparently the author means that although the duly instructed guest will only partake moderately of the abundance before him, what he eats is as good as the rest. His portion will be equal to the whole as regards quality, though inferior as regards quantity.

3. If thou sit with a glutton, eat with him, then depart (?).

If thou drink with a drunkard, accept [drink], and his heart shall be satisfied.

Refuse not meat when with a greedy man. Take that which he giveth thee ; set it not on one side, thinking that it will be a courteous thing.

4. If a man be lacking in good fellowship, no speech hath any influence over him. He is sour of face toward the glad-hearted that are kindly to him ; he is a grief unto his mother and his friends ; and all men [cry], ' Let thy name be known ; thou art silent in thy mouth when thou art addressed ! '

5. Be not haughty because of thy might in the midst of thy young soldiers. Beware of making strife, for one knoweth not the things that the God will do when He punisheth.

The Vizier caused his sons and daughters to be summoned, when he had finished the rules of the conduct of men. And they marvelled when they came to him. Then he said unto them, ' Hearken unto everything that is in writing in this book, even as I have said it in adding unto profitable sayings.' And they cast themselves on their bellies, and they read it, even as it was in writing. And it was better in their opinion than any thing in this land unto its limits.

Now they were living when His Majesty, the King of Upper and Lower Egypt, HEUNI, departed, and His Majesty, the King of Upper and Lower Egypt, SENFÔRU, was enthroned as a gracious king over the whole of this land.

Then was Ke'gemni made Governor of his City and Vizier.

IT IS FINISHED.

APPENDIX

THE Instruction of Amenemhê'et I. is here given as a contrast to the foregoing. It is a Testament, however, rather than an Instruction. and contains more historical matter than didactic, It is written in a terse and pointed style, combined with the parallelism and antithesis which was the prevailing vehicle of poetic thought in Egyptian. The rank of its author and the exceeding bitterness of his mood make it a document of great interest. There is no reason to doubt its authenticity.

This King was the founder of the glorious Twelfth Dynasty, a period which has been called the Golden Age of Egypt. He ruled from about 2778-2748 B.C., and, although he describes himself as over-lenient, was really one of the most vigorous and powerful of all the Sons of the Sun who for five thousand years wore the double crown of the Two Egypts.

The circumstances in which the new dynasty arose are not known; nor have we any other record of the attempt on his life, here recounted.

In the twentieth year of his reign he associated his son, Senwesert I., with him in a co-regency which lasted ten years. From §8 we gather that the attempted assassination took place just before the dual rule ; while the Instruction was evidently penned shortly before the writer's death. The 'house' referred to is presumably his pyramid-tomb, called Ke'-nôfer-amenemhê'et. *Amenemhê'et is exalted and good.* The site of this building is not known.

This Instruction was popular as a school exercise in the 'New Kingdom,' and we possess several copies or parts of copies. There is no good text for the latter part (§§ 12 *ff*), which is corrupt in such MSS. as contain it

I have used the critical text of Mr. Griffith, published in the *Zeitschrift für ägyptische Sprache*, 1896.

It is hoped that the Bibliography will be useful to students of the books of Ptah-hotep and Ke'gemni.

B. G. G.

THE INSTRUCTION OF AMENEMHÊ'ET

BEGINNETH here the Instruction made by the Majesty of the King of Upper and Lower Egypt SEHÔTEP-'EB-RÊ', Son of the Sun AMENEMHÊ'ET, the Justified.[1] He speaketh thus in discovering words of truth unto his Son, the Lord of the World :

1. Shine forth, he saith, even as the God. Hearken to that which I say unto thee : that thou may reign over the land, that thou may govern the world, that thou may excel in goodness.

2. Let one withdraw himself from his subordinates entirely. It befalleth that mankind give their hearts unto one that causeth them fear. Mix not among them alone ; fill not thine heart with a brother ; know not a trusted friend ; make for thyself no familiar dependents ; in these things is no satisfaction.

3. When thou liest down have care for thy very life,[2] since friends exist not for a man in the

[1] A ceremonial title applied to deceased persons, analogous to our "the late." "Justified" is not an exact rendering, but it is usual, and will serve.

[2] Literally, *heart*.

67

day of misfortunes. I gave to the beggar, and caused the orphan to live; I made him that had not to attain, even as he that had.

4. But it was the eater of my food that made insurrection against me; to whom I gave mine hands, he created disturbance thereby; they that arrayed them in my fine linen regarded me as a shadow; and it was they that anointed themselves with my spices that entered my harem.

5. My images are among the living; and my achievements are among men. But I have made an heroic story that hath not been heard; a great feat of arms that hath not been seen. Surely one fighteth for a lassoed ox that forgetteth yesterday; [1] and good fortune is of no avail unto one that cannot perceive it.

6. It was after the evening meal, and night was come. I took for myself an hour of ease. I lay down upon my bed, for I was weary. My heart began to wander (?). I slept. And lo! weapons were brandished, and there was conference concerning me. I acted as the serpent of the desert. [2]

7. I awoke to fight; I was alone. I found one struck down, it was the captain of the guard. Had I received quickly the arms from his hand,

---

[1] An allusion to the people of Egypt, whom he had freed from the foreign oppressors.
[2] *i.e.* he remained quiet but watchful.

I had driven back the dastards by smiting around. But he was not a brave man on that night, nor could I fight alone; an occasion of prowess cometh not to one surprised. Thus was I.

8. Behold, then, vile things came to pass, for I was without thee; the courtiers knew not that I had passed on to thee [my power], I sat not with thee on the throne.[1] Let me, then, make thy plans. Because I awed them not I was not unmindful of them; but mine heart bringeth not to remembrance the slackness of servants.

9. Is it the custom of women to gather together assailants? are assassins reared within my palace? was the opening done by cutting through the ground? The underlings were deceived as to what they did.[2] But misfortunes have not come in my train since my birth; nor hath there existed the equal of me as a doer of valiance.

10. I forced my way up to Elephantinê, I went down unto the coast-lakes;[3] I have stood upon the boundaries of the land, and I have seen its centre. I have set the limits of might by my might in my deeds.

11. I raised corn, I loved Nôpi[4]; the Nile begged of me every valley. In my reign none

[1] Referring to the co-regency with his son.
[2] Referring to the attempted assassination.
[3] The limits, south and north, of his kingdom.
[4] The god of corn.

hungered; none thirsted therein. They were contented in that which I did, saying concerning me, 'Every commandment is meet.'

12. I overcame lions; I carried off crocodiles. I cast the Nubians under my feet; I carried off the Southern Nubians; I caused the Asiatics to flee, even as hounds.

13. I have made me an house, adorned with gold, its ceiling with *lapis lazuli*, its walls having deep foundations. Its doors are of copper, their bolts are of bronze. It is made for everlasting; eternity is in awe of it. I know every dimension thereof, O Lord of the World!

14. There are divers devices in buildings. I know the pronouncements of men when inquiring into its beauties; but they know not that it was without thee, O my son, Senwesert; life, safe and sound, be to thee—by thy feet do I walk; thou art after mine own heart; by thine eyes do I see; born in an hour of delight, with spirits[1] that rendered thee praise.

15. Behold, that which I have done at the beginning, let me set it in order for thee at the end; let me be the landing-place of that which is in thine heart. All men together set the White Crown on the Offspring of the God, fixing it unto its due place. I shall begin thy praises when in the Boat of Ra. Thy kingdom hath been from primeval time; not by my doing,

[1] Or, unborn souls (*hmmw*).

who have done valiant things. Raise up monuments, make beautiful thy tomb. I have fought against him whom thou knowest; for I desire not that he should be beside thy Majesty. Life, safe and sound, be to thee."

IT IS FINISHED.

AN EXPLANATION OF NAMES OCCURRING IN THIS BOOK.

AMENEMHÊ'ET . *The God Amôn is to the fore.*

HEUNI . . *I have smitten.*

ISÔSI . . Of unknown meaning.

KE'GEMNI . *I have found a soul; or, A soul is found for me.*

PTAH-HOTEP . *The God Ptah is satisfied,* alluding either to the belief that to beget a child was pleasing to the God, or to the dedication of the child to the God.

SEHÔTEP-'EB-RÊ' *Contenting the heart of the God Ra.*

SENFÔRU . . *The beautifier.*

SENWESERT . Of doubtful meaning; connected with *The Goddess Wesert.*

Other spellings of these names are: *Amenemhat; Huna; Assa, 'Esse'; Ptahhetep; Sehetepabra, Rasehetep-ab; Seneferu; Usertesen.*

72

BIBLIOGRAPHY

Brugsch, H. *Hieroglyphisches-demotisches Wörter-buch* . . . vols. v.-vii. Leipzig, 1880 *ff.* Contains explanations of many difficult passages.

Budge, E. A. W. *An Egyptian Reading Book.* London, 1888. Second edition, with transliteration into italics and vocabulary, London, 1896. Contains the most convenient transcript of the P.P. Follows throughout that of Virey (see below). For some amendments see Griffith in Proc. S.B.A. (below). The first edition is more accurate (for this text) than the second. The vocabulary needs revision.

Chabas, F. *Le plus ancien livre du monde ; étude sur le papyrus Prisse.* Revue archéologique, première série, xv. anno. Paris, 1857. Contains a discussion of the text, etc., and partial translation.

Chabas, F. *Le papyrus Prisse.* Zeitschrift für ägyptische Sprache. Berlin, 1870. Discusses the meaning of various words.

Chabas, F. *Le plus ancien livre du monde ; étude sur le papyrus Prisse.* Bibliothèque orientale, vol. ii. Paris, 1872. The work of 1857 recast.

Dümichen, J. *Les sentences de Kakemni.* Les Bibles et les initiateurs religieux de l'humanité, vol. ii. part i. Paris, 1884. Contains a translation of Kg.

Griffith, F. L. *Notes on Egyptian Texts of the Middle Kingdom*, iii. Proceedings of the Society of Biblical Archæology, vol. xiii. London, 1890. Discusses the text, correcting some previous errors in transcription. Translation of Kg. and §§ A, B of Ph.

Griffith, F. L. *Egyptian Literature.* A Library of the

World's Best Literature. New York, 1898-9. Contains translation of many sections.

Heath, D. I. *On a MS. of the Phœnician King Assa, ruling in Egypt before Abraham : A Record of the Patriarchal Age ; or, The Proverbs of Aphobis,* B.C. 1900 ; *now first fully translated. Monthly Review.* London, July, 1856. The first 'translation' of Kg. and Ph. Afterwards issued as a pamphlet, London, 1858.

Lauth, F. J. *Der Autor Kadjimna vor 5400 Jahren.* Sitzungsberichte der kgl. bayer. Akademie der Wissenschaften. München, 1869, ii. Contains an analysis of Kg.

Lauth, F. J. *Der Prinz Ptah-hotep über das Alter : Ptah-hoteps Ethik.* Sitzungsberichte der kgl. bayer. Akademie der Wissenschaften. München, 1870, ii, Heft i, Beilage. Contains analysis and translation into Latin and German of the greater part of Ph.

Mahaffy, J. P. *Prolegomena to Ancient History*, part ii. London, 1871. Contains translations from Lauth's rendering.

Myer, T. *The Oldest Books in the World.* New York, 1900. Contains Virey's translation and notes.

Petrie, W. M. F. *Religion and Conscience in Ancient Egypt.* London, 1898. Contains translations of many sections by F. L. Griffith.

Prisse d'Avennes, E. *Facsimile d'un papyrus égyptien, trouvé à Thèbes, donné à la Bibliothèque Royale de Paris, et publié par E. P. d'A.* Paris, 1847.

Rawnsley, H. D. *Notes for the Nile, together with a Metrical Rendering of the Hymns of Ancient Egypt, and of the Precepts of Ptah-hotep (the Oldest Book in the World).* London, 1892.

Revillout, E. *Les deux préfaces du papyrus Prisse.* Revue égyptologique, tome vii. Paris, 1896. Contains translation of Kg. and § A of Ph.

Revillout, E. *Les Maximes de Ptah-hotep.* Revue égyptologique, tome x. Paris, 1902. Contains translation and text of Ph.

Virey, P. *Études sur le papyrus Prisse, le livre de Kagimna et les leçons de Ptah-hotep.* Bibliothèque de l'École des Hautes-Études, fasc. 70. Paris, 1887. Contains complete translation and elaborate discussion of the text ; also glossary.

Virey, P. *The Precepts of Ptah-hotep* (*the Oldest Book in the World*). Records of the Past, new series, vol. iii. London, 1890. Contains a translation of Ph.

Printed by Hazell, Watson & Viney, Ld., London and Aylesbury.

The following mystical pictures are not related to this book.

They have been included for your enjoyment.

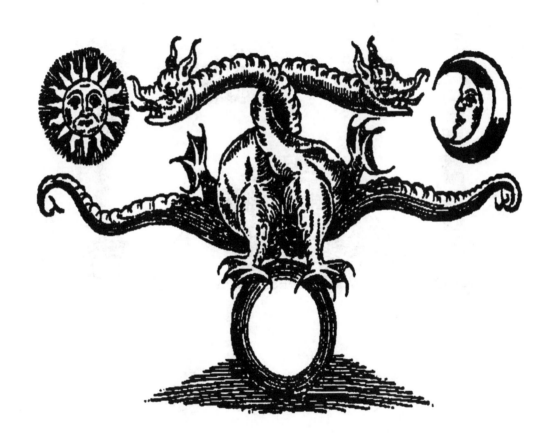

Pictures 1

Pictures 2

FAITH, HOPE, AND CHARITY.

Pictures 4

Pictures 5

ALCHYMIA
(From Thurneysser's Quinta Essentia, 1570)

 Pictures 6

Pictures 7

Pictures 8

Pictures 9

Assyrian Type of Gilgamesh

Pictures 10

Pictures 11

MASONIC APRON PRESENTED TO GEN. WASHINGTON
BY MADAME LAFAYETTE.

THE GOLDEN WHEEL

Pictures 15

Pictures 16

Pictures 17

Pictures 18

Pictures 19

Pictures 20

Pictures 21

Pictures 22

Pictures 23

Pictures 24

IMMA NUEL

In hoc signo vinces

Pictures 25

Pictures 26

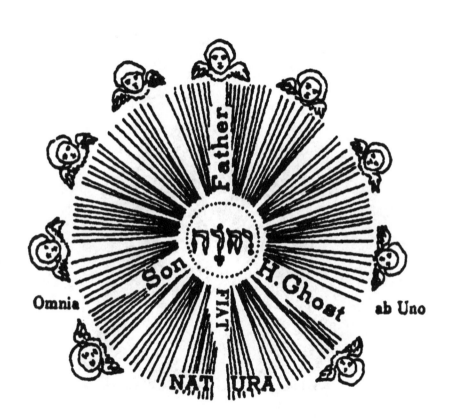

Pictures 27

Pictures 28

Pictures 29

Pictures 30

CPSIA information can be obtained
at www.ICGtesting.com
Printed in the USA
LVHW061405060223
738776LV00014B/937